My Family's OK

My Family's OK

BY DAVID ALLEN SORENSEN

AUGSBURG Publishing House • Minneapolis

MY FAMILY'S OK
A Young Christian Book for Boys

Copyright © 1987 Augsburg Publishing House

Scripture quotations unless otherwise noted are from the Holy Bible: New International Version. Copyright 1978 by the New York International Bible Society. Used by permission of Zondervan Bible Publishers.

Photos: Dave Anderson, 12, 20, 38, 78, 92; Robert Maust, 46, 64; D. Michael Hostetler, 70.

Library of Congress Cataloging-in-Publication Data

Sorensen, David Allen, 1953–
    My Family's OK : a young Christian book for boys / David Allen Sorensen.
        p.   cm.
    Summary: A collection of fifteen stories depicting boys with family stories that relate them to their brothers, sisters, parents, and God. Includes a Bible quotation and prayer with each story.
    ISBN 0-8066-2301-2
    1. Children's stories. American. [1. Family life—Fiction.
2. Christian life—Fiction. 3. Short stories.] I. Title.
PZ7.S718My   1987
[Fic]—dc19   87-31013
                                                    CIP
                                                   AC

Manufactured in the U.S.A.   APH 10-4633

1 2 3 4 5 6 7 8 9 0 1 2 3 4 5 6 7 8 9

For my grandmothers,
Anna and Anna,
and to God who, showing great wisdom,
gave me grandmothers with the same
first name so I would never
be forced to choose which to honor
with a dedication first!
I love you both very much.

Special thanks to my spiritual family at
Marynook Ecumenical House of the Lord in
Galesville, Wisconsin,
for your love and a special place to write.

Contents

About This Book

Stop for a moment and think of how much your family affects your life.

How much time do you spend with your parents? Your brothers and sisters? How often do the decisions they make for their lives affect your life? Do you live where you live because it was your choice, or because it was a family decision?

Who do you look most like from your family? Do you enjoy the same things to do as other people in your family?

Nowadays, families come in as many different forms as there are flavors of ice cream at the store. What flavor of ice cream is most like your family? Why?

In this book, we will take a look at some boys who have family stories that are funny, stories that have some heartache, and stories that sound like they could have happened to you.

9

And while we are talking about families, we should remember that as Christians we are part of the Family of God. So we will see what the Word of God has to say about what the boys in these stories go through.

At the end of each story one of the characters in the story shares a prayer with you. It's an important part of the whole story. Then, if you want to set the book down once in a while to rest your eyes, you may want to do the action ideas that finish each chapter.

When you think about your family—and God's Family—may you always be able to say, *MY FAMILY'S OK.*

"How can you say to your brother, 'Let me take the speck out of your eye,' when all the time there is a plank in your own eye?"
—Matthew 7:4

•

"What will I steal next? You'll have to wait and see, dear diary."
—*Roberta*

Diary in the Dark

Jimmy slipped the table knife into the crack next to the doorknob of his sister's room. He slid and wiggled the knife expertly as he pulled steadily on the door. The bolt eased over and the door, though still in the lock position, swung open.

"Just like magic," he whispered to himself. "I'm getting good at this."

Jimmy shut the door with a quick, smooth motion. There was only a hint of a squeak and no click at all.

The room had its own peculiar smell. *Heavy and too sweet,* Jimmy thought. Without hesitation, he moved toward the bureau with all the little bottles and cases lined up neatly on top. Once again, he curled his lip and thought, *Why do girls work so hard to out-stink each other? Yuck!*

11

My Family's OK

He opened the top drawer, lifted the socks on the left and pulled out a glossy, black book. The diary.

Jimmy turned expertly to the middle of the book where he found the latest entry. He leaned toward the shaded window to catch the setting sun, and read:

Dear Diary,

Today, I stole a gold necklace at the shopping center.

What? Jimmy could hardly believe what he was reading.

I don't know why I did it. Now that I have it in the small drawer of my jewelry box—

Jimmy dropped the diary and tore into the jewelry box on the top of the bureau next to all the perfume. "Oh, no," he moaned as he caught the glitter of gold. "She really did it." He went back to the diary and flipped pages to find his place.

Now that I have it in the small drawer of my jewelry box, I don't know what I'm going to do with it. I can't wear it. Mom and dad would know it was stolen. Maybe even Jimmy. I might sell it. Or I could melt it down so nobody would be able to identify it.

I don't know why I did it, but I know that it made me feel more excited and alive than I've ever felt before. But I must never tell a soul about this, not even Cheri.

What should I steal next?

You'll have to wait and see, dear diary.

Love,
Roberta

13

Jimmy checked for the date at the top of the entry. *Yesterday's date,* he realized. *What am I going to do?*

•

Jimmy was reading the funnies left over from Sunday when Roberta got home that evening.

"Hi, Jimmy," she said. "Where's mom and dad?" She dumped three bulging bags on the writing desk, then threw the car keys in the desk drawer. She had gotten her license just a few months previously.

"At Carney's," Jimmy replied. "They said they will be late. Where ya been?"

"Oh, nowhere. We had late practice, then I went to the mall to do some shopping. You wouldn't believe the bargains I got."

Jimmy swallowed hard. "Were you with Cheri?" he asked.

"No. I know I'm with her all the time, but I like to do some things on my own. Why do you ask?"

"Oh, nothing." Jimmy stuck his nose back in the paper, but for the first time in his life he didn't find the funnies funny. Roberta gathered her bags and rustled off to her bedroom.

She'll get caught. Her name will be in the newspaper. Everybody will know. It's just . . . wrong! All of these thoughts came to Jimmy as he tried to get up enough nerve to go in and tell Roberta he knew. *But then she will also know that I broke into her room.*

In the end, Jimmy decided to wait and see if she would strike again. In fact, he suspected that she had already done so. Jimmy had to know for sure as soon as possible.

The next morning, Jimmy found that the usual routine was changed. For the first time, Roberta had gotten permission to get a ride to school with Cheri instead of taking the bus. "Be careful," their mother had said. "And make sure Jimmy is out the door and hiking before you lock up the house. I've got an eight o'clock meeting or I'd see you both off."

Jimmy was out and hiking all right, but he only went around the block before doubling back and cutting through Pearson's yard just as Cheri and Roberta pulled out of the driveway.

In less than two minutes, with table knife in hand, Jimmy was holding the diary. The newest entry said:

Dear Diary,

I did it again! This time it was an expensive blouse and sweater. It was easy. I wore them out under my jacket.

These first two have been too easy. What would be harder? Maybe next it will be a computer or even a car!

What will I steal next? You'll have to wait and see, dear diary.

Love,
Roberta

●

That evening, Jimmy shot baskets in the driveway while his parents worked together to get supper ready. He wanted to talk with Roberta as soon as she got home.

I have to do it, he decided. *I am the only person who knows what's going on. It always sounds so corny when someone else says it, but I know that even though she will be mad at me, she will thank me some day.* Jimmy thrust out his chest with the power of Truth running through his veins as he saw Cheri's car pull around the corner and into the driveway.

Roberta popped out, then pulled a medium-sized box out of the back seat. It had a picture of a computer on the side.

"Thanks, Cheri," she said. "Pick me up first thing tomorrow again, OK?"

"Sure, and don't forget to watch the special on TV tonight. What's-his-hunk is on. If he sings that song again, I'll die." Cheri rolled her eyes up and pretended she was having a heart attack. The car rolled slowly into the street. Suddenly realizing that she was moving, Cheri braked with a jerk, accidentally hit the horn with her elbow, covered her red face with one hand, and drove off with a wave.

"She's crazy," Roberta said simply.

"Dangerous, you mean. Where'd you get the computer?" Jimmy asked.

Roberta paused and looked at him with a curious expression. "It's a long story," she finally said.

Roberta was no sooner past the swinging side door of the house when Cheri came around the corner again and pulled up to the curb.

"I forgot to tell Robbie to bring my gold necklace to school tomorrow," she said. "I got it from my rich aunt and uncle and they're visiting us this weekend, so I'd better have it around. Tell her for me, OK?"

Jimmy cocked his head to the side for a moment, then said, "A flat, gold necklace with two little nuggets in front?"

"That's it. And you'd better keep your hands off it, Jiminy Cricket, or else!"

"Where'd Roberta get the computer?"

"Ask her yourself."

"She said it was a long story."

"Let me give you a hint," Cheri said. "There's a certain someone at school who likes computers but he likes Robbie better than computers and would lie, cheat, or steal to have her pay attention to him."

"He stole it for her?"

"No, silly. He gave her his own beloved computer to use for a while and in return she has to go out with him on Friday. I'll never understand it; he has too many pimples and not enough money for my tastes."

"So she's just borrowing. . . ."

"Remind her about the necklace," Cheri called out as she accidentally squealed the tires with another jackrabbit start.

Jimmy stood in the driveway holding the basketball as the roar of the old car faded. Things were falling into place. He punted the ball into the garage, then turned and went into the house where he found that the barbecued chicken and mashed potatoes were already on the table.

"Sit up," his father said. "Let's eat."

They had scarcely finished the table prayer when Jimmy said, "Robbie, how come you never wear that gold necklace?"

"You stinking little sneak!" she exploded.

"Roberta!" her mother exclaimed, obviously surprised at the outburst.

"Mother, he has been breaking into my room to read my diary. But I haven't known it for sure until now. There's no other way he could have known about the necklace. I caught him and now . . . ."

"Cheri told me," Jimmy said innocently. He put a pat of butter into the ditch he had made in his mashed potatoes, and said, "Pass the salt and pepper, please."

"Cheri told you what!" Roberta demanded.

"She came back a few minutes ago and asked me to remind you to return the necklace you borrowed. She needs it for the weekend."

Roberta suddenly looked like she just forgot everything she had ever known.

"I guess . . . I guess . . ." she stammered.

"I guess you owe Jimmy an apology," her father said.

Jimmy thrust out his chest very slightly and waited.

"I'm sorry, Jimmy," she said.

"No big deal," he replied. He put on his best whipped-puppy look but wondered briefly if he should have acted a little more mad.

"That sounds better," their mother said. She smiled kindly at Jimmy who gave her the droopy-eyed look that says I-know-I'm-a-good-boy. "Now," she continued, "since we are getting to the bottom of things, would someone please tell me why all of our table knives are getting scratched up?"

Jimmy finished his supper in silence. It was a very long time before he again thrust out his chest and felt the power of Truth running through his veins.

Jimmy's prayer: I can't tell them about what I did yet, Lord. Maybe some day. Is that OK? Amen.

Action idea: Think of short answers to these questions:
● What animal did Jimmy most remind you of?
● How long should Jimmy wait before telling Roberta the truth?
● Would James 5:16a help Jimmy to make up his mind on telling the truth?

My Family's OK

"Greet one another with a brotherly kiss."
—Romans 16:16 TEV

•

"Never trust a skunk."
—Gary

Kissy-Kissies Are for Sissies

Gary opened the back door of his house and headed for the refrigerator.

"Yuck," he said out loud after he spied all the leftovers from his sister's so-called *special* recipes. "A whole week of her cooking was plenty."

"What, Gary? Talking to the ice box gremlins again, are you?" His sister, Beth, stood in the doorway with her hands on her hips just like their mother did when she scolded them.

"Sure," Gary replied. "They say they want me to order out for Chinese food tonight. They're tired of fighting with the cockroaches over who has to eat your leftovers."

Gary snared the last piece of two-day-old pizza, slammed the refrigerator door too hard, then flipped on the cold water tap.

"If you stick your face under that spiggot and slurp again—" Beth began.

21

Gary slurped, then ran as a knotted dish towel thumped him in the middle of his back.

Gary's dad had gone for a full week to a convention in Texas and, after a lot of coaxing, Gary's mother had decided to go with him . . . on one condition. Gary's sister, Beth, had to spend her spring break home from college taking care of him.

"Come on, mom!" Gary had complained, "I'm not a baby any more. I can take care of myself." But he knew she would never buy it.

"I know, Gary," his mother had replied, "but I'll feel better knowing Beth is here."

Gary was old enough to know that arguing was hopeless.

A car horn sounded outside and Gary heard the familiar roll of the tires in the driveway.

"They're here," Beth yelled from the kitchen.

Gary spun around in the hall and jogged back through the kitchen, following Beth past the swinging screen door.

"Hi ya, kids," his dad said through the open car window. "Great trip. How did you two get along?"

"Hi, dad," Beth said. "Aside from his taste in music, fine." She laughed.

"Beth! Gary!" Gary's mother looked tan and rested as she stepped from the car. She walked first toward Beth.

"Hi, Honey," she said affectionately, giving Beth a kiss on the cheek. "Hi, Gary," she echoed, reaching to do the same to him.

Gary stepped back uncomfortably.

"Yah, well, I'd better help you with the suitcases. Looks like you bought a lot of stuff," he mumbled.

"Gary, where's my hug?" his mother coaxed.

"Mom, I'm not a kid anymore," he answered. He chose the two heaviest looking suitcases and hefted them toward the house.

"That's OK, Gary," she said behind him. "I understand."

"Way to go," Beth said as she opened the door for Gary. "Now you've hurt her feelings."

Gary didn't even give Beth a dirty look. He knew what he had done. But he also knew that he hadn't meant to hurt his mother. *Kissing your mom and dad is for kids and maybe for older girls like Beth,* Gary thought. *But not for me. Doesn't anyone understand that?*

Gary dumped the suitcases in his parents' bedroom.

I've got to do something to make them understand, he thought, *but what?*

●

"A doghouse is nothing more than a big birdhouse, right?" Gary asked of his friend, Elliot.

"Sure, Gary," Elliot said with a smile creeping out the sides of his mouth.

"No, I'm serious," Gary said.

"Why do you ask? Are you going to buy an ostrich?"

"Just answer the question."

"Well," Elliot began, "birds and dogs are completely alike . . . except that one flies, has wings, a beak, feathers, claws, eyes on the side of its head, hollow bones so it's light, lays eggs, and eats worms. So I guess their houses must be pretty much completely alike too."

"Very funny."

"Does your dog, Cleo, eat worms now?"

"Let me start over," Gary said, finally realizing how silly the conversation had sounded so far. "I am going to build a doghouse for Cleo. It's something that dad and mom have wanted to do for a long time so Cleo can sleep outside sometimes. I figure that everyone will know, you know, that I . . . sort of . . . love them, if they see all the work I am willing to do."

Elliot raised his eyebrows slightly. "So that is what this is all about," he said. "Why don't you just give them all a hug like we do all the time in my family?"

"I can't."

"You mean you won't," Elliot replied.

Gary looked thoughtful for a moment. "I have to get going on that doghouse. I've never done this before, but I built a birdhouse in scouts last year, so I'll just make this a big birdhouse. Want to help?"

"Big Bird house? You mean like on Sesame Street?"

"You're hopeless," Gary said, then they went into the garage to bring out the wood and the tools and the birdhouse for a model.

24

•

"Let's just sit in here and not say anything about the doghouse until someone notices it first," Gary suggested to Elliot as they each ate a bowl of ice cream at the kitchen table.

"Hi, Honey," his mother said as she led the shopping expedition in from the garage. His mother and father dumped the grocery bags on the counter. "Did you two find enough to keep you occupied on a hot Saturday afternoon?"

Just then Beth burst in the other kitchen door from the backyard.

"It's awful, it stinks, there's some kind of huge birdhouse or something in the backyard and . . ."

This time she's going too far, Gary thought. He was about to yell back at her when she finished her sentence.

". . . and a skunk inside the thing just tried to spray me when I poked my head in the door."

"What!" exclaimed Gary.

"We're going to have to burn that thing out there, whatever it is," Beth concluded.

Gary and Elliot looked at each other seriously, then laughed loudly.

"All that work," Gary said.

"I know an easier way," Elliot replied.

Gary got up from the table and walked around the room, hugging each of his family members (even Beth) warmly.

"It *is* easier," Gary said. Then he turned back to Beth. "But sister, I really should tell you that that skunk didn't miss you completely."

She suddenly ran for the bathroom.

"We didn't raise a boring family," Gary's dad said to Gary's mom. "Now what's this about a huge stinky birdhouse?"

Gary's Prayer: *Dear God, you wouldn't believe how hard it is to show people that you love them. On the other hand, when I think of how hard Jesus worked to show people how much you love us, I guess maybe you know all about that. Amen.*

Action Idea: Build a birdhouse as a gift to someone you love. But when you deliver the gift, be sure to give a hug too. Gary would like that!

"A heart at peace gives life to the body,
but envy rots the bones."
—Proverbs 14:30

•

*"I guess living with my family is better than
getting poked in the eye with a sharp stick, but I
wish I lived with John's family instead."*
—Derek

Wanted: An Exciting Family

"What's for supper?" Derek asked as he sauntered into the kitchen. Spying the familiar narrow box, he said quickly, "No, let me guess: macaroni and cheese, hamburger patties, and frozen peas cooked just six minutes in the microwave."

"Hit the microwave for me, Mr. Wise Guy," his mother said in a tired voice, "and tell the others supper is in six minutes."

"Here's the world famous chef about to whip up another world famous dish," Derek said. He scooped up a damp dish towel, took aim, and snapped at the start button on the microwave. A hit! The light went on inside and he could see the peas begin to come alive.

"You never told me you didn't like this supper," his mother said with a touch of hurt in her voice.

"I never said I didn't like it. It's just so . . . so . . . I don't know."

"Go get the others," she said with a sigh. "And I think your dad has a surprise for you."

"Could it be a saddled ostrich in the garage? Maybe a treasure map turned up in the attic. What if . . . ?"

"You're impossible," his mother called after him as she flipped the spattering hamburger patties.

"Hi, Jason; hi, Susie," he announced to the twins as he plopped into the bean bag chair next to the bookcase. They continued to stare past his shoulder at the television. When he leaned forward into their line of sight, they leaned left to look around him. "Nice to see you, too," he continued. "Too bad a monster ate your preschool, isn't it?"

After a few seconds, Jason turned and said, "Huh?" Susie was still staring.

"I said, supper's in five minutes."

Jason didn't respond. He just turned his face back toward the television with his mouth still open from saying "Huh."

"It's not your fault that you're this way," Derek whispered as though they were listening to him. "We've all eaten too much macaroni and cheese with hamburger patties and peas . . . oh, never mind."

Behind the newspaper, his father said, "Is that you, Derek?"

Really now, he thought, *who else would come in here without ringing the doorbell first and do a Derek Duncan imitation?*

28

"Supper's in four minutes, dad," Derek replied.

"OK. Say, I've got a surprise for you."

"That's what mom said."

His father laid the newspaper on his lap. "What do ya say we take the weekend to go to grandma's cabin at the lake and help her put the dock in, maybe do a little fishing? It's Memorial Day weekend coming up, you know."

This isn't a surprise, Derek wanted to say. *We always put the dock in on Memorial Day weekend, and we never catch anything worth keeping in that dinky lake.*

"Sounds good, dad," Derek said.

"Great," his father said. "It'll be just you and me." Then he picked up the newspaper and turned back to the sports section.

Derek settled back in the floppy bean bag chair and glanced at the TV. A blue cow puppet was doing the Hawaiian hula while a band of duck puppets played bagpipes.

Rolling his eyes, he threw his head back, just missing the bookcase, and waited for the microwave timer to ting.

●

"Shut the door and keep the animals out of the house!" John's father yelled at Derek and John from the family room. "And be quiet! Oh, hi, Derek."

"Hi, Mr. Yates." Derek liked the balding fix-it man. Sometimes he was swamped with lawn mowers and toasters to fix; otherwise, he worked on one crazy invention after another. The creations that came from these hours brought in more than enough money to make ends meet. But, in any case, he always quit working at 4:00 to watch his game shows.

"Boys, come in here," John's mother called from the kitchen. "I've been waiting for you to get home. One of you stand here and the other on the other side of that green canvas." Two bright lights were aimed at the canvas which hung from the wall.

What now? Derek wondered.

"When I say go, I want Derek to throw that squash to John with panache. I will shoot it in mid-air."

Derek thought it sounded crazy and dangerous, and he was embarrassed to ask what *panache* meant, but he was willing to try.

"She means she'll shoot it with her camera, Derek," John said. Derek was relieved but he still thought *panache* sounded messy. "She's been working on some advertising photos for a grocery store all week."

Mrs. Yates got her camera set up, then said, "Ready . . . go!"

Derek threw the squash too high, as it turned out, where it hit the hook on which the canvas was hanging. Suddenly, the whole world seemed to be falling down; canvas, squash, dirty dishes from the counter, the telephone, John (as he dived to catch the small aquarium which was home to Gomer and Obed), and finally the tall light stands with the thousand watt bulbs that exploded when they hit the floor.

There was a moment of silence as John peeked out from under the canvas with Gomer and Obed safe in the two inches of water that hadn't spilled. Then, "QUIET!!" John's dad yelled from the other room. "The guy's going for $25,000 in here!"

Mrs. Yates, talking as though nothing out of the ordinary had just happened, whispered, "Can you stay for supper, Derek? We're having cooked sushi sticks and chef's surprise."

John interpreted: "She means we're having fish sticks and leftovers."

Somehow, Derek knew it would be an interesting—even exciting—supper.

"HE WON!" Mr. Yates yelled from the family room.

●

"I'd trade with you in a minute, if I could," Derek said. "My family's so boring."

"You wouldn't last a week in my family."

"I'd love it."

"There's lots of yelling."

"It makes things exciting."

"Dad never talks to me."

"Because he's working on all those great inventions."

"Derek . . . I'd trade places with you in a minute if I could."

"You wouldn't last a week in my family," Derek said with a grin.

"I'd love it," John replied.

"It's so boring."

"They love you no matter what."

Derek stopped grinning. "You know," he said. "You're right."

John nodded.

"Do you want to come along to the lake this week-end with my dad and me? He isn't so boring when he gets away from work and newspapers."

"Sure!"

"Don't count on catching anything but dinky sun-fish and throwing them back. And you'll get your legs ice cold when we put the dock in the lake. And grandma will put us to bed with about three or four prayers and wake us up with pancakes and bacon."

"Sounds pretty exciting to me, Derek," John answered.

Derek's prayer: Help John to like his family better. Amen.

John's prayer: Help Derek to see the good in his family like I do. Amen.

Action idea: Draw three circles on a large sheet of paper, then draw a picture of what your family would look like if it was a three-ring circus.

"Father, I have sinned against heaven and against you. I am no longer worthy to be called your son."
—Luke 15:21

●

"Trouble is spelled J-U-S-T-I-N."
—Justin

Trouble Enough to Share

Justin didn't take time to kick off his wet boots or even pull the inside door shut tight behind him. He took to the wide staircase two steps at a time, sweeping past his 10-year-old brother, Jeff, swung left at the top and burst into Patrick's room.

"I gotta talk," he puffed with a loud whisper that sounded more like a muffled yell. Justin poked his head back out the door, looked both ways, then closed the door swiftly.

"So talk." Patrick typed to the end of a sentence, then turned around from his place at the corner desk. He had been spending a lot of time there studying during this last week of his high school career.

"I'm in trouble, Pat. Mom and dad are going to kill me."

"You're all wet, Justin."

"No, really! They'll kill me when they hear—"

"I mean that you are dripping all over the hardwood floors. Mom will kill you."

"That's what I'm saying," Justin said, taking off his raincoat and throwing it on Patrick's bed.

"Oh, maaaan," Patrick wailed. "Now you're getting my bed all wet."

"Shhh!" Justin's frantic look finally got Patrick's attention.

"So what is it this time, little brother?" he asked.

"Ryan and I were in the school yard hitting golf balls just now. . . ."

"In the rain?"

"I know, we could have been hit by lightning. We were going to quit as soon as we saw any."

"A golf club makes a great lightning rod," Patrick said. "Attracts electricity like I attract women."

"Girls, you mean . . . did you know Rhonda McMillan likes you? . . . anyway, that's not the important part."

"So? . . . she's too young . . . get to the important part."

"So I hit the greatest nine-iron of my life. Used my best ball. It went way over a hundred yards, bounced on the sidewalk by the benches, went another fifty yards—"

"—and went through one of the huge windows in the cafeteria."

"How did you know?"

"Bobby Salter's big brother did the same thing when I was in sixth grade."

"You're kidding!"

"He didn't get caught. Did you?"

Justin suddenly looked very uncomfortable. "Not really but sort of."

Patrick snorted, "That's what I like, a man who is sure of himself."

"What I mean is, Ryan saw me do it. No one else . . . just Ryan."

Patrick looked thoughtfully at the floor, then asked, "Do you think he'd tell?"

"I don't know, Pat. I don't think so. . . ."

"But. . . ."

"But you're going to think I'm dumb for saying this."

"Hey, don't worry about spoiling what I think of you; I already think you're the original Dumbo."

Justin smiled weakly at the insult. He knew Patrick was just trying to make him feel good.

"It's just that I don't want Ryan to think I'm a total jerk, you know, dishonest." This time it was Justin's turn to look at the floor. He stirred his toe in the growing pool of water beneath him. "Dumb, isn't it. I don't want to get caught or anything, but part of me thinks I should. What would you do, Pat?"

"I'd enlist in the Army."

"Yeah, right . . . but what would you really do?"

"I'll tell you, but that doesn't mean you have to do it. Each of us is different, OK?"

"Sure."

"All right," Patrick said. "You said that was your best ball. Well, I'd go back to school to get it. With the shot that you hit, it deserves to be made into a trophy."

"But I'd have to own up and pay for the window. It's probably hundreds of dollars," Justin argued.

"It would be an expensive trophy, that's for sure."

"But mom and dad. . . ."

"They'll forgive you. They won't like paying for most of it, there may even be some yelling, but they will forgive you."

"But how do you know for sure?"

"You don't know half the dumb things I've done, Squirt."

Justin grinned.

"On second thought, maybe you do. Anyway, they know how to let things blow over."

"I need to think about this for a while. I'll make a decision before tomorrow," Justin said. "Until then, keep this a secret, OK?"

Patrick shrugged and said, "Sure. You really trusted me by telling me all this, you know."

"I guess I didn't even think about it," Justin replied. "You've always been someone I could talk to."

"Well, I want to tell you something too, but you've got to promise not to tell anyone for a while."

Justin nodded. Then, as Patrick told him the secret, Justin could do nothing but nod some more. Later, closing the door to his brother's room, Justin felt the sting of tears he hadn't wanted his brother to see.

•

Justin typed the last few words of his letter to Patrick, tucked it into the airmail envelope and stood up from his place at the corner desk. Then, on second thought, he sat back down and added a note to his letter:

P.S. By the way, I moved into your room when the Army sent you to Germany. It's cool, but I'd give it up in a minute to have you back. I never knew how hard it would be not having an older brother around.

Just then, Jeff barged in. "Justin, I gotta talk to you!"

Justin smiled a faraway smile, then turned and said, "So talk."

Justin's prayer: Thank you, Lord, for insurance companies and understanding principals and parents who forgive . . . and thank you for brothers. Amen.

Action idea: Write a letter to someone you like. Tell them how you really feel. Then, if you're curious how the Bible story that this chapter began with ended up, turn to Luke 15:11-32. It's quite a story!

My Family's OK

"The more you know, the more it hurts."
—Ecclesiastes 1:18b TEV

•

*"I'm kind of nervous. I've never been to see a
social worker before. Where do we start?"*
—*Charlie*

The First Session

COUNSELOR: Have a seat over there, Charlie. I should tell you right away that I just turned on the tape recorder so I can go back and evaluate our first session together.

CHARLIE: We're being recorded right now?

COUNSELOR: Yes. There's the mike. When this hour is over, I'll have the secretary type up our conversation. Is that all right with you?

CHARLIE: Why not? If you think it might help.

COUNSELOR: I think it might help.

CHARLIE: I'm kind of nervous. I've never been to see a social worker before. Where do we start?

COUNSELOR: Any other 12-year-old would be nervous, too. Let's talk about the divorce.

CHARLIE: I guess that's why I'm here.

COUNSELOR: I've met with both your parents, separately and together. They're nice people, but I don't think they want to be married to each other anymore.

39

CHARLIE: I know. They both say they're going to go through with it.

COUNSELOR: They also both say they're concerned about you, you know.

CHARLIE: *(Pause)* If they were so concerned about me, they wouldn't get a divorce.

COUNSELOR: What do you mean?

CHARLIE: I don't think they love me anymore.

COUNSELOR: What have they done to make you think that?

CHARLIE: The divorce.

COUNSELOR: I see. Anything else?

CHARLIE: No.

COUNSELOR: Have they done anything recently that lets you know that they do, in fact, love you?

CHARLIE: I suppose so.

COUNSELOR: For instance. . . .

CHARLIE: Mom is hugging me a lot more these days. And she's trying to make our house happy, in spite of . . . you know.

COUNSELOR: The divorce.

CHARLIE: Exactly. And dad is taking time for me more than he usually does, even though he doesn't live at home anymore.

COUNSELOR: So you see him regularly?

CHARLIE: Almost every other day.

COUNSELOR: And how does being with your parents, now that they're apart, make you feel?

CHARLIE: *(Pause)* Happy and sad at the same time, I guess.

COUNSELOR: What do you mean?

CHARLIE: Well, there isn't so much yelling and stuff. By themselves, they seem happier than they were before.

COUNSELOR: And that makes you happy?

CHARLIE: Yes, sort of. But I'm sad, too, though I don't show it much in school in front of the other kids.

COUNSELOR: Do any of your friends know what your family is going through?

CHARLIE: Not yet. It's still pretty new so it hasn't gotten around. I'll know when it does; they'll tease me.

COUNSELOR: You're an only child, aren't you?

CHARLIE: Yup.

COUNSELOR: So if you don't have any brothers and sisters, and your friends don't know about this, and your parents are both hurting . . . who does Charlie get support from these days?

CHARLIE: Grandma, you, and God.

COUNSELOR: I heard your grandmother was living with you. Is she special to you?

CHARLIE: When I was a kid she was special because she brought me presents.

COUNSELOR: And now that you're almost a teenager?

CHARLIE: She talks to me. She's known mom since she was born, you know, and she knew dad when he was in high school, so she understands things better than I do.

COUNSELOR: She sounds like a good one to have around.

CHARLIE: And she is getting me pre-prayered for the divorce.

COUNSELOR: Prepared in what way?

CHARLIE: No, pre-*prayered*. We are praying for both mom and dad. We figure that even if they don't get back together our prayers together will help me to do better.

COUNSELOR: Does praying help you?

CHARLIE: Yes, but it's kind of hard to explain what it does for me. I guess I'm not a really good prayer but I am getting to know God better.

COUNSELOR: Sounds like an important thing for you to continue with your grandmother.

CHARLIE: We will. *(Pause)* I have a question.

COUNSELOR: Go ahead.

CHARLIE: You have to be honest with me about this.

COUNSELOR: I'll be as honest with you as I can be, Charlie.

CHARLIE: Do you think they would still be together if I hadn't messed up so much at home and school?

COUNSELOR: Uh. . . .

CHARLIE: What I mean is, I didn't used to make my bed all the time and I fussed about having to take out the garbage or sweep the garage floor. Do you think I caused some of the arguments that mom and dad had? I worry about that. I wish I had been better . . . then maybe they wouldn't be . . . you know. . . .

COUNSELOR: Getting a divorce?

42

CHARLIE: Exactly. Did they say anything like that about me?

COUNSELOR: Charlie, I told them that it is common for kids to think those things when parents get a divorce. And you know what they said?

CHARLIE: What?

COUNSELOR: They both said that you were the very best thing about their marriage, and you are likely to be the reason that they continue to see each other once in a while.

CHARLIE: They said that?

COUNSELOR: Yes. Charlie, if you want my honest opinion, I think things would have been even worse if they didn't love you so much.

CHARLIE: Oh. I have another question.

COUNSELOR: Shoot.

CHARLIE: Do I really have the right to choose who I want to live with?

COUNSELOR: The judge at the hearing will ask your opinion, and your opinion counts for a lot.

CHARLIE: But how am I going to choose? I can't hurt either of them by choosing the other.

COUNSELOR: Charlie, I can't answer that for you. You know what?

CHARLIE: What?

COUNSELOR: I think that's something for your grandmother and you to pray about.

CHARLIE: You know what?

COUNSELOR: What?

CHARLIE: I think you're right.

Special Note to the Reader: Charlie never had to choose which parent to live with. They decided to try working things out in the marriage, after all. Charlie's father moved back into the house one week after Charlie's first session.

Grandma's (and Charlie's) prayer: Dear God, thank you for answering our prayers in the way that we hoped. And thank you for bringing Charlie and me closer to each other and for bringing both of us closer to you during those prayer times. Amen.

Action idea: There isn't a family on earth that is happy all the time. Pray for families that you know are going through tough times, then thank God for all the good and healthy times in your family.

"For everything God created is good, and nothing
is to be rejected if it is received with
thanksgiving."
—1 Timothy 4:4

●

"I'm thankful for spit; really, I am."
—Jacob

Spit, Spit, Spit

"When you first go outside in the morning, what
do you do?"

"Spit."

"As soon as you step out of a car, what do you
do?"

"Spit."

"After you tasted Rosie's cookies this afternoon,
what did you do?"

"Spit."

"Right on the kitchen floor!" Jacob's dad fairly
shouted.

"A mistake," Jacob replied. "I thought I was closer to the sink."

"The point is, you know you're doing all this, so
why don't you stop it?"

"Stop what?"

"Spitting! Aren't you listening to me?" His father finished with one of those my-son-is-from-another-planet looks.

"I can't help it," Jacob said.

"Can't help what?" Mr. Osborn asked.

"Spitting! Aren't you lis. . . . " Jacob started to say, mimicking his father. He clapped a hand over his own mouth. "Sorry," he said behind the hand, "that just kind of slipped out."

"Just like the spitting, you can't help it, I suppose."

Jacob could tell the chewing-out was over. His dad's eyebrows had finally come back down to join the rest of his face. *Here comes the final piece of advice,* Jacob thought, *then I can go play baseball.*

"Promise me you'll apologize to Rosie."

"I will, dad," Jacob said.

"Before you go play baseball."

"Sure, dad," Jacob said.

"And no more spitting."

Jacob took a deep breath before he answered.

"Not even if the candles burn down too far at the dinner table and get the napkins on fire and there's no water in the drinking glasses and the faucets don't work and the only water in the whole house is in the toilet? Can't I even spit then?"

"Only then," his father conceded.

It was a small victory, Jacob thought, *but it was something.*

47

•

The following Saturday, the entire Osborn family—from all over the state and even out of state—met at the nearby Slag County Park for the once-every-five-years family reunion.

"Why do you spit all the time?" his cousin, Rachel, asked only 15 minutes after arriving at the park.

Jacob made some quick calculations. *She couldn't have seen me spit more than three or four times so far. And who gives her the right to get on my case when I haven't seen her in five years?*

"It's a disease," Jacob replied.

"Come on," she groaned in disbelief.

"Really! My body builds up too much fluid and this is the only way I can relieve the pressure short of having surgery."

Rachel eyed him slyly.

"Doctor says I am supposed to spit at least two quarts a day."

"Two quarts!" Rachel exclaimed. "That's a half gallon."

"At least," Jacob insisted.

"Oh, yeah? If it's a disease, what's it called?"

Jacob thought quickly. "I don't know how to spell it," he explained, "but it's pronounced *globulitis.*"

"Oh," Rachel said.

The rest of the family reunion was uneventful, but Jacob noticed some of the out-of-towners whispering and pointing at him later in the afternoon.

48

Spit, Spit, Spit

•

Jacob tried for weeks to quit spitting. But he couldn't quite catch himself until it was too late. The best he did was to stop it from clearing his chin, but that was a messy success. So he took to muttering to himself after every spit: "Come on, Jake," "filthy habit," and things like that.

His parents didn't think that this was an improvement. In fact, they worried even more about the way he would spit-and-mutter, spit-and-mutter.

The showdown with both parents finally came. But Jacob was prepared.

"We're just worried that there may be some reason why you can't quit doing this," his mother said.

Maybe there really is a disease called globulitis, Jacob thought.

"We're concerned," his dad said.

"Do you remember the pastor's sermon this last Thanksgiving?" Jacob asked. He was met with blank stares. Jacob continued, "The pastor said we should learn to be in the habit of thanking God for everything, even things that we don't normally think of." He had gone too far to stop. "Well, I'm thankful for spit."

Silence.

"I see," his father said.

"Think about it, dad. Without spit your mouth would taste dry and dusty all the time, and your food wouldn't get digested the way it should."

"I see," his mother said.

"And I've been thinking," Jacob continued. "I don't think too many people thank God for earlobes or doorbells or those plastic tips on the end of shoelaces. Do you know how hard it would be to lace your shoes if you didn't have those?"

"I get it. You think we should be thankful for spit, too," his mother said.

"Why not?"

"Jacob," his father said, "God made spit and we can be thankful about it, but he made it for a certain purpose."

This time it was Jacob's turn to say, "I see."

"Spit is great. God made all of it. But don't you think it does what it was made to do best if it remains in our mouths?"

"That's all any of us can hope to do," his mother added. "Just to do what we were created to do."

"That's fair," Jacob said.

"And right now the place for your spit is in your mouth, and the place for you is in bed," his father said with calm eyebrows.

Jacob really didn't spit after that conversation . . . much.

Jacob's prayer: Thank you, God, for all the things I have never really thanked you for before. Amen.

Action idea: Make a list of 20 things that you suspect nobody has ever thanked God for before. Then thank God for them!

"In doing this, you will heap burning coals
on his head."
—Romans 12:20b

•

*"I kind of like the sound of that—heaping burning
coals on Terry's head . . . and best of all,
it's in the Bible!"*
—Wendell

Fright Night

"I can walk you home," Andy said at the door. "It's really gotten dark while we were eating supper."

"Stupid," replied 11-year-old Wendell Wilson III, "then you'd have to walk home in the dark instead of me."

"Oh, I hadn't thought of that," Andy said. "Anyway, don't even think of going past the graveyard at night."

"Stupid, I'd have to go ten thousand miles out of my way to miss it. That's how you get to my house. Remember?"

With a laugh and a wave, Wendell left the lighted warmth of Andy's house. He quickly became as dark as the moonless night around him.

"Call me when you get home," Andy called out behind him. "And quit calling me stupid!"

Call him when I get home! He's starting to sound like my parents, Wendell thought. *That's stupid, too!*

Wendell tripped momentarily over something soft on the dark asphalt road.

It's dark and sticky and about the size of a . . . dead cat! Wendell hopped onto the grass and wiped the toe of his shoe vigorously.

The smell of the dead cat receded as he jogged for a few blocks, but he slowed down again as he reached the cemetery.

The massive oak trees surrounding the cemetery always seemed to Wendell to reach over the low stone fence to grab at people walking on the sidewalk. Wendell loved to jump at their branches during the day but almost always chose to walk on the street at night.

This time was different.

That stupid dead cat might have scared me, but dumb trees don't, he almost said out loud. He jumped the curb and was ready to jump again to swipe at a low branch when he saw something white out of the corner of his eye.

He glanced left in time to see what looked like a large, white bundle fall out of one of the 80-foot oaks. It grew longer as it fell until it appeared taller than Wendell, then it swooped out of its dive and headed straight towards him.

Wendell wouldn't have been more suprised if the dead, smushed cat had risen from its own blood to bite his ankle.

The fluttering, white phantom dropped below the level of the stone wall briefly, but suddenly surged over the top, gaining speed and coming right at Wendell.

As he ducked, a startled cry frozen in his throat, he felt the wind of the thing's passing. He thought again about yelling, but decided not to as he saw it bounce and scuffle across the street. It came to rest in a heap by the bushes, a long rope trailing behind it.

Laughter erupted from his left.

Then a voice: "You said you wouldn't let go of the rope. You probably ruined my mother's sheet and scraped up the basketball inside it."

Wendell recognized his brother Terry's voice. Terry was barely a year older than Wendell but was two years ahead in school. Terry's favorite hobby? Scaring Wendell.

Terry and his friend, Mark, vaulted the stone fence and switched on their flashlights in Wendell's face.

"We knew you'd be coming home from Andy's house right after supper," Terry said smugly, "so we just waited. It was a great ghost, wasn't it?"

"But we didn't hear you yell, Wen-DELL," Mark taunted.

Wendell decided not to let Terry and Mark have the satisfaction of knowing how scared he had been. "I'm not afraid of sheets, Stupid," he replied. "I sleep on them every night."

"Then how come you are still crouching down?" Terry whined. "Lose something?"

In the shock of the moment, Wendell had forgotten that he had ducked all the way to the ground.

"Cleaning dead cat off my shoe," he replied. "They get sticky, you know."

•

Saturday was a plotting day.

Wendell spent several hours trying to concoct the perfect trick to pull on Terry.

In between the plotting, he looked up words in the dictionary, like "revenge: to inflict punishment or injury in return for a wrong done."

Wendell liked the sound of that definition so well that he read it three times. Then, because he was so sure that he had a right to his revenge, he actually took down a Bible and looked in the subject index in the back for the same word.

When he looked up some of the passages that used the word *revenge*, he didn't find what he expected to find.

"Do not take revenge, my friends," it said in Romans, Chapter 12, "but leave room for God's wrath, for it is written: 'It is mine to avenge; I will repay,' says the Lord. On the contrary: 'If your enemy is hungry, feed him; if he is thirsty, give him something to drink. In doing this, you will heap burning coals on his head.' "

This is a little confusing, Wendell thought. *I'm not supposed to take revenge . . . but if I am nice to him*

*by giving him something to eat and drink it will heap
burning coals on his head. This is very, very confusing. . . .*

"I'll do it!" he said out loud.

That evening, Wendell made a special trip to the
grocery store with some of his own money. He
bought a six-pack of Terry's favorite soft drink and
one of Terry's favorite frozen pizzas with double
topping and double cheese.

Later, as he was cutting the cooked pizza and
pouring the sodas over ice in tall glasses, Terry wandered into the kitchen.

"What are you up to?" he asked.

"Hungry, Terry?" Wendell asked.

"If I say yes you won't give me any and if I say
no you won't give me any so I won't say anything.
I know how you get after I scare you good, like last
night."

"Thirsty, Terry?" Wendell asked, ignoring his
comments.

"Why? What did you put in the glass?"

"You can have your pick of any of this. It's all
your favorite stuff," Wendell said.

Terry could resist no longer.

That night Wendell and Terry ate and drank together.

And sometime after the pizza went in the oven
but before Terry finally apologized, Wendell quit
imagining live burning coals on Terry's head.

Wendell forgave Terry.

All things considered, one might call that a miracle!

Terry's prayer: Dear God, I felt like a hotheaded bully when Wendell made that great pizza for me tonight. I feel bad about the way I've been treating Wendell. Really, I think he's an OK brother. I just don't act like I think he's an OK brother. Help me to act the way I really feel. Amen.

Action idea: Do something nice to someone who has been unkind to you.

"No insults or obscene talk must ever come from
your lips. Do not lie to one another."
—Colossians 3:8b-9a TEV

•

*"I've said some pretty awful things about
my family in front of the others.
I wonder if I really meant them. . . ."*
—Jeff

My Family's OK

The second hand on the kitchen clock swept away
another minute as Jeff stared at the blank sheet of
wide-lined paper. *Oh, maaan . . . why did I wait so
long to start this thing?* Jeff asked himself for the
fourth time since eight o'clock.

"By the end of this week," Miss Gall had said on
Monday, "I want each of you to turn in your paper
describing your family. Two pages. This is a creative
writing assignment so be creative; don't just tell me
their names and ages. Remember, you must turn it
in first thing Friday morning without fail. *No ex-
cuses.*"

It was Thursday evening panic time.

He grabbed his #3 pencil with a slap. *I'm going*

to just write whatever comes to my mind, he resolved.
Miss Gall calls this stream-of-something-or-other writing.

He wrote:

> My Family
> by Jeff Morrow
> I wish I didn't have to write this stupid paper for
> Miss Gall's stupid class—

"I can't write that!" he said aloud, crumpling the
sheet into a wad. "So much for stream-of-whacha-
callit writing."

He started again:

> My Family
> by Jeff Morrow
> My family's OK, I guess. I mean, they're not so
> great or anything. They're just . . . OK, I guess.

Jeff dropped his head onto the table with a clunk.
*Two pages of saying my family's OK? I'll never be able
to do it. I can't even think of ONE reason why I think
they're OK right now.*

It had been one of those weeks at home that nobody should have to go through.

It started with the creamed baby onions at supper
on Monday. Seven-year-old Alvin had gagged down
a few with the help of at least half a gallon of milk.
The milk hadn't helped. It just made all the more
for him to vomit later. All over the kitchen table.

That's why I haven't been able to write this paper,
Jeff thought. *The table has stunk all week.* But he
knew the excuse was feeble. Jeff's dad had scrubbed

it for an hour with soap and baking soda and vinegar and bleach and a couple other things.

On Tuesday the cat got hit by a car. Jeff had watched in horror as his mother stomped a shovel on its neck to stop the twitching. He never knew his mother had it in her. She didn't even cry.

"Good-bye, Mouser," she had said, handing Jeff the shovel. "Bury him, Jeff."

Fat ol' Mouser was always my special friend. For mom to just . . . well . . . it all seemed so cold and horrible for him to get it like that. Jeff stroked his own neck tenderly. *No wonder I couldn't concentrate on my homework assignment on Tuesday.*

On Wednesday the postal carrier had brought him a birthday present from great grandmother. *So what if it was three months early? They didn't have to go and hide it! Now Alvin is going around singing with that nya-nya whine of his, "I know where they hid it, I know where they hid it." Sometimes I think I'd like to take a shovel and. . . . Well, maybe not.*

Wednesday was also the day that Jeff was grounded by his father because of The Chipmunk Incident. . . .

Stacey was too young to know the difference between when Jeff was kidding and when he was not. While she was riding her tricycle in the driveway that afternoon, she had had fun chasing a lone chipmunk in and out of the open garage. As Jeff strolled up the drive after school he said casually, walking past her, "You can get away with that as long as there's just one chipmunk, Stacey, but if they ever start grouping in 20 or more be careful they don't just carry you away and bury you with the nuts."

Stacey hadn't reacted at all. She just stood there trying to count to 20 on her fingers. That's why Jeff had been surprised when, a few minutes later, Stacey came shrieking into the house with two grubby fingers held up shouting, "Twenty chickmunks! There's twenty chickmunks! Ahhh!!!"

It's hard to write a homework assignment on your family after you've been grounded, Jeff thought.

Jeff looked at the sheet in front of him. "My family's OK . . . I guess," it said. *Did I write that? Did I mean it? OK compared to what? I guess living with them is better than being a bug on the floor at a square dance, like grandpa used to say. I mean, at least they didn't name me Joe Nerd or something. They're OK compared to—*

Tap! Tap! Tap!

Jeff jumped in his chair and looked sharply to his left. Pug had pressed his thick lips to the kitchen window from the outside and inflated his cheeks. With eyes bugging out, he actually looked ready to explode.

Jeff couldn't help but laugh; Pug could do that to him faster than anyone else in the world.

In a second, Pug had let himself in the back door, grabbed a handful of leftover stale popcorn from a bowl on the counter and joined Jeff at the kitchen table.

"I've gotta stay here tonight, Jeffrey Baby. Temperature's pretty hot at my house tonight."

"Your parents?"

Pug nodded.

"They know you're here?"

"Yup. I'm supposed to have one of your folks call one of mine to clear things."

Jeff thought Pug was taking it all rather well. "What's happening with your parents, Pug? Yelling? Hitting even?"

"Worse," Pug replied.

Jeff was sorry he had asked.

"Much worse." Pug wrinkled his nose and said, "Kissing!"

"I thought you said the temperature was getting hot over there."

"It is. It's kind of hard to watch TV with two old people smooching in the big chair next to you."

"Aren't parents a pain sometimes? I mean, really?" Jeff asked with a glance at his barely-started paper.

Pug looked like he was about to agree, but he got a thoughtful look on his face and said, "You serious?"

"About parents being a pain? Sure, and the whole family thing, too. What a pain! Right, Pug?"

"If you're really going to be serious on me tonight, I'd say no, not really."

Somehow, Jeff was sure Pug wasn't kidding this time.

"I don't get it," Jeff said. "You complain about your family all the time. You're usually worse than the rest of the gang, in fact. Just this morning you said—"

"Jeff," Pug started, "we do all that just to be funny, don't we?"

"Do we?"

"That's why I do it . . . to be like the other kids and to get a laugh. I thought you knew that."

"You mean you're not mad because your parents are kissing in front of the TV?"

"You kidding? Why should I be against kissing? Did I ever tell you about the time I kissed Greta last summer when—"

"But you always say it's not cool to like your parents and family and stuff."

"Jeffrey, it's not cool to *say* you like your parents and family and stuff but that doesn't mean that you can't *really* like them. You just do it. You gotta like them or else . . . or else . . . or else how could you ever write that stupid paper for Miss Gall's class? You've written it, haven't you?"

Jeff just stared. *I wonder if everyone thinks the same as Pug. I've said some pretty awful things about my family in front of the others. I wonder if I really meant them. . . .*

"I suppose you're going to tell me you think my family's OK too," Jeff droned in a bored tone, but really he was quite interested in how Pug would answer.

"Your family's more than OK," he replied. "I can think of a dozen reasons why I like to come over here."

After pausing to let his mind adjust to Pug's new attitude, Jeff said, "If you name a few of those reasons I have a feeling I'll finally be able to write this paper."

"My mouth would work better if it was lubricated with some chocolate ice cream, don't you think?" Pug said as he stood and peeked into the freezer.

Jeffrey didn't answer. While Pug began dishing up a bowl for each of them, he took out a new sheet of paper and wrote:

My Family
by Jeff Morrow
My family's OK! Here are a dozen reasons why I think so—

Jeff's Prayer: I'm feeling kind of mixed up, God. I thought I was embarrassed to be part of this family, but maybe I never really meant it very much. Am I part of your family too? I guess I'm not really embarrassed about that either but I'm not ready to tell anyone about that just yet. Let's talk about that later. Thanks for understanding. Amen.

Action Idea: Christians are part of at least two families: your earthly family and your heavenly family. Pick one of them and describe a dozen reasons why you think it's OK to be part of that family.

"We must help the weak, remembering the words the Lord Jesus himself said: 'It is more blessed to give than to receive.'"
—Acts 20:35b

●

"Sara said airily, 'Our brother, the saint.' 'Our brother with cold oatmeal for brains, you mean,' Lisa scoffed."

The Strangest Choice

"A whole anything?"

"A whole anything."

"A whole anything at all?"

"A whole anything on the face of the earth as long as I eat it."

"Eat what?"

"The whole-anything."

"This is getting confusing."

"I can have a whole anything-I-want to eat on my birthday," Lee said. "Last year it was a whole pizza, before that a whole batch of deep-fried shrimp, a whole chicken, a whole lobster, and when I was a kid it was stuff like a whole box of *Alphabits*. It's great."

"So what will you have this year?" Marc asked.

"I'm not sure. It's not as easy as it used to be because

I want something that I really love but I don't want to have the same things I had before."

"I wish we did that in our family," Marc said. He kicked up the kickstand of his bicycle and started rolling slowly. "But my mom says we spend too much on extras for ourselves already."

"Besides," Lee replied, "you have six kids in your family and we have only three. It would cost you twice as much."

"Anyway, I hope I can come and get in on your whole-anything dinners every year, so I can get as many of them as you do." At the end of the driveway, Marc suddenly stopped the bike, feet still on the peddles, and pulled the front wheel off the ground, trying to spin a full three-sixty on his back wheel. "Happy birthday!" he cried, then he kicked one foot to the ground to break a fall. "Well, I didn't quite make it."

"That's OK," Lee said, "it's not quite my birthday yet either. I have one more day to decide what kind of a whole-anything I want for dinner tomorrow."

"I hear elephant is very tasty," Marc laughed, then he was off.

Lee thought about whole-anythings all evening. He thought about a whole five-pound box of chocolates while he was eating supper. He thought about a whole package of crispy-fried bacon while he helped with the dishes. He even thought about a whole gallon of chocolate-fudge-brownie-nut ice cream with caramel topping while he was watching television. He was starting to feel a little sick just thinking about it all. He couldn't get the image of bacon bits in the chocolate ice cream out of his head.

Suddenly, he knew.

He called Sara and Lisa from the kitchen where they were doing their homework and he called his parents from upstairs where they were cleaning closets.

Nobody wanted to leave what they were doing but they all came when they heard the excitement in Lee's voice.

"I know what I want for my birthday dinner," Lee said when they were all seated in the living room.

"I hope we can still get it in time for tomorrow, Lee," his dad said. "It had better not be anything too exotic."

"You said that we can each have a whole-anything to eat on our birthday, right?" Lee asked with a voice that said he had something up his sleeve.

"Yes," his mother said, "as long as it is possible for us to do."

"A whole anything at all?"

"A whole anything on the face of the earth as long as you eat it," Sara said. "That's what they've always said. So what is it, Lee?"

"On my birthday. . . ." He paused, enjoying the drama of the moment. He knew that his two sisters enjoyed this part of birthday celebrations at the Reynolds house as much as he did.

"Yes?" Lisa said to help him get going again.

"On my birthday. . . ." He repeated, then he pulled out a Kleenex to blow his nose.

"It's going to be next year's birthday before you get it if you don't hurry up," his father clipped.

Lee walked to the other side of the room just to make them all the more eager to hear what he had to say.

"On my birthday . . . now don't think I'm dumb for saying this because it is a little bit unusual, but you said that it could be anything on the face of the earth, right?"

"RIGHT!" all four people shouted. They were enjoying this as much as Lee.

"On my birthday," Lee said once again, "I want a whole village to eat."

"You want to eat a whole village!" his mother exclaimed. "And what do you want to go with it? A river made of lemonade and a swimming pool of catsup?"

"Our brother, the cannibal!" Lisa said to Sara with dramatic horror and an arm up to shield her from Lee.

"I didn't say I want to eat a village," Lee explained patiently. "You said I could have a whole-anything to eat, so I want a whole village to eat on my birthday. I want them to eat! I want us to send the money to Africa that we would otherwise spend on my birthday dinner. I just heard on the TV that a whole village can eat for a day on what it costs the average American family to eat for one meal at a restaurant."

"You want the whole village to *eat,* not the whole village to *eat,*" Lisa said with exaggeration.

"Lee, I think we all understand," Mr. Reynolds said. "But are you sure that is what you want?"

"Yup!" Lee barked. "The day after tomorrow I'll regret it, but right now I feel pretty good about doing this."

As Sara and Lisa wandered back to the kitchen, Sara said airily, "Our brother, the saint."

"Our brother with cold oatmeal for brains, you mean," Lisa scoffed.

The following morning, Marc rolled up on his bike while Lee was out front clipping the hedge.

"So what's it going to be for the birthday meal?" he called out before he had even stopped.

"You know how they said I could have a whole-anything to eat? Well. . . ."

Mengistu's prayer: *O God of all, with our hearts we thank you for this meal, this gift from our Christian brothers and sisters in the world who know that so many starve in my land. Bless them and give us also the chance to serve them in ways that we are able. May we all be one in the church on earth. Amen.*

Action idea: Think of a way that a family tradition in your house can be enlarged to include the family of people on earth. Sound too hard? Lee did it!

My Family's OK

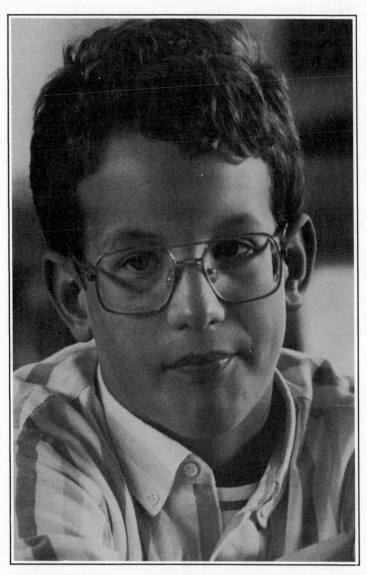

"God sets the lonely in families."
—Psalm 68:6a

•

*"We call the police in 10 minutes. Do your best.
The school is depending on you . . . and so is
Caryn."*
—The Principal

Temporary Sister

Steve Foster was an only child—except when he wasn't an only child—which happened every now and then. Sometimes Steve was an older brother who helped fix the bottles for twin babies; sometimes he was a younger brother of a brother who drove too fast and stayed out too late. And sometimes he didn't even have his own room if there were too many brothers and sisters at one time.

Steve's home was a short-term foster home. The social worker that they worked with, Kay, chuckled when she told people about her best place, the Foster foster home.

It was on a Friday that Caryn came striding through the front door while Steve was watching TV.

"The name's Caryn and I'm three years older than you," she said.

THUD!! She dropped her single over-stuffed suitcase in the center of the room.

"That's Caryn with a *C* and a *Y*, Caryn!" she emphasized.

"Hi," Steve said, rolling over on his other side to watch her, "I'm Steve; that's Steve, spelled S-T-E-V-E-9, but the nine is silent." He grinned.

She didn't. In her most business-like voice Caryn said, "If we both happen to be home for lunch from school—and I understand that will happen frequently—we will watch my soap opera on Channel 10."

"That's all right, I don't watch—" Steve began, but she interrupted.

"I get the bathroom for 30 minutes every morning *without* being interrupted, understood?"

"That's all right, I only need—" he began again.

"And if I ever catch anyone listening in on my phone calls I'll call the police!"

Steve thought of all the temporary brothers and sisters he had had in the past. Some had fit in and some hadn't. *This one won't last,* he felt sure.

"The number's 9-1-1," he said.

"The numbers in your name?" she asked. "That's retarded."

"No, the number to call the police." Steve rolled back over to watch his TV show.

"Oh," she said. After standing silently for a minute she added, "Your hair would be really cute if you parted it differently, blow it dry, and comb it back instead of just down."

"Thanks . . . I think," he mumbled. "Welcome to the family."

"It's only temporary," she answered.

Steve had to swallow hard so as not to say "Good!"

•

"Mr. Shisler," the intercom hissed.
"Yes?"
"Is Steve Foster in your class?"
Mr. Shisler looked around the room until his gaze fell on Steve.
"Yes, he is," Mr. Shisler replied, "but I hope you're not going to ask him to leave because we are in the middle of a very important test."
There was a pause.
"The principal insists on his coming down to the office immediately," the secretary said firmly.
"It had better be an emergency," Mr. Shisler said.
Another pause.
"Just ask him to come as soon as he can. Thank you, Mr. Shisler."
"You're welcome, Mrs. Greene. Steve, you heard the lady. Here's your pass. Drop your test off now and see me after school. We'll work something out."

•

"This is kind of embarrassing, Steve," Mrs. Valdez, the principal, said. "I hope you won't let this get around or we may have others try it."
"How did Caryn do it?" Steve asked.
"I just left my office for one minute to get a cup of coffee and she barricaded herself in there. She must have the desk in front of the door."

73

"Won't she leave?"

"She won't talk to us," Mrs. Valdez replied. "We can't even be certain that she hasn't done damage to herself or the room because she closed all the curtains."

"I hardly know her myself," Steve said, thinking back on the three short weeks she had been hogging the bathroom and telephone. He suspected that she had been making quite a few long-distance calls, but that would end really fast once the bill came, he knew.

"We just want you to talk with her to see if she's OK and to ask her to come out . . . before we have to call the police," Mrs. Valdez rattled off quickly. "If she comes out now we will just send her back to her classroom like nothing happened."

"Sure," Steve replied reluctantly. "Could you leave me in this outer office by myself? I don't know if she will talk if anyone else is here."

"Of course." Mrs. Valdez turned around at the door. "We call the police in 10 minutes. Do your best. The school is depending on you . . . and so is Caryn."

She closed the door behind her.

What do I say? What do I say? What do I. . . . He walked up to the door between the two offices. "Say, Caryn, it's your limp-haired almost-brother, Steve."

He thought he heard a slight shuffle inside.

"You gonna talk to me?" he asked.

"No," Caryn said from the other side of the door.

"What is it that you're not going to say to me if you don't talk to me?" Steve asked.

Silence.

"Are you OK in there?" he asked.

Silence.

"Well, you only have about nine minutes before they call the police, so you had better talk."

Longer silence.

"I'll tell you what," Steve began, "I'll talk to you and if you don't talk back to me I'll make up your part of the conversation, too. OK?"

He was glad that nobody was in the room to hear what he was about to do.

"OK, here goes," Steve said. "Hi, Caryn. Hi, Steve. What are you doing? Oh, I'm all locked up in the principal's office. That's a funny thing to do. Well, your talking to yourself is kind of funny, too. So we're both acting dumb today. I guess so. It must run in the family. I'm not part of your family. Mom and dad think you are. Why do they want me to come live with them anyway? Because they think everybody deserves to have a family and they want to be yours for a little while. They won't be able to handle me and they'll send me back to the social worker. That may be true if you keep acting like this but it won't be their fault because at least they are trying."

Steve paused, feeling kind of dumb for what he was trying to do. *She's probably laughing at me right now.*

"I'm trying," came the small voice on the other side of the door.

"Are you really?" Steve asked her.

"I'm trying because I'm tired of not having anybody love me," she said with a sigh. "It's too lonely."

"It must be lonely being locked in the principal's office. . . ."

"It is," she said sadly. "I'll come out on one condition."

Steve looked up at the clock. Only two minutes to go before they would call the police.

"What's the condition?" he asked. "You'd better make it fast."

"I'll tell you after you come in here for a few minutes," she replied mysteriously.

Steve thought it over. He went to the other door, opened it a crack, and said, "She'll come out in a few minutes, so please don't call the police."

"We know," Mrs. Valdez said. "We've been listening to the whole thing on the intercom."

Steve rolled his eyes back in his head and shut the door, embarrassed that they had been listening. *I should have guessed!* he thought.

Exactly three minutes later, Steve and Caryn emerged from the principal's office. Caryn was smiling like she was just back from a walk around the park on a sunny day. Steve looked sheepish but dapper with his new hair style, parted differently and combed back instead of straight down. The blow dryer would have to wait until he got home.

Mr. and Mrs. Foster's prayer: Dear Lord, we hope we're doing the right thing by getting out of the short-term foster care program and into longer-term care. We just feel that we can do more good by helping fewer kids but for longer periods of time for a while. Help us to love Caryn more and more in the next years and thank you for a son like Steven who seems to understand her even better than we do. Amen.

Action idea: God places us in families (there are many kinds) for a reason. To see the difference, pretend for a moment that you had no family or foster family or adoptive family at all and answer the following:

- Where would you live?
- Would you feel safe?
- What would your life be like?

"Every good and perfect gift is from above."
—James 1:17a

•

"That gift in the dark brown wrapping was the best gift you gave our family this year!"
—Mick

Wrapped in Shades of Brown

"So, what are the surprises for Christmas this year?" Mick asked with the curiosity all 10 kids felt.

"I wan' 'prises," little Sammy called from a mouthful of mashed potatoes.

"Won't it be like the other years with all our family traditions?" asked Ruth, the eldest.

"I wan' fam'ly tadishuns an' more taters!" Sammy demanded from the high chair.

"Sue, give Sammy another scoop," their father said. "All right. Everybody listen up."

Twenty-two ears—belonging to 10 kids and the mother that washed the ears regularly—were all turned to listen. Christmas was serious business to them all.

"There isn't a lot of extra money this year," Mr. Barnes began. "There'll always be enough to feed you, and you will all get something for Christmas . . ."

The group let out a collective sigh.

". . . but you're going to have to be creative in giving presents to each other."

"I wan' taters!"

"You can each give Sammy a potato for Christmas," their dad said. "That will make Sammy happy."

"Sappy hammy," he replied with a grin as the others laughed.

Their mother came in right on cue, "You can make things for each other, you can find something beautiful in nature to give, you can check out books and posters from the library for each other and make sure you are responsible to get them back on time, you can give something that you have already enjoyed for a while and want to let someone else use; oh, there are lots of things you can do without spending money. You could even give out free coupons offering to do each other's chores."

Groan. . . .

Mick sat back and stretched his feet out under the table, surprised that he didn't kick into a knot of other legs. "Is that the only thing you meant when you said there'd be surprises?" he asked.

"Well, another thing is we're not going to kill a tree for Christmas this year," his father replied. "Maybe never again."

"No treeee . . . !" half the kids wailed.

"I didn't say we wouldn't have a tree," he said quickly. "I said we wouldn't kill one. Ruth and Mick and I dug one up from the north side of the old homestead a month ago and wrapped the roots in burlap. After we are done using it, we'll toss it behind the barn to freeze and then plant it near the house in the spring when the ground gets soft again."

"Why all the trouble to do something like that?" Stephen asked.

"So we don't celebrate Christ's birth with a tree's death. Besides, this world is going to be in big trouble if people keep killing off trees like we've been doing."

"Trees make oxygen for us to breathe," Ruth told the younger ones.

"Silly, trees don't make oxygen; they just make apples and oranges," Morgan said with arms folded on his chest.

"And taters," added a little voice.

"The final surprise," their mother said, "is that we are going to have a very special guest with us for Christmas dinner."

"Santa Claus!" the younger ones cheered.

At that, Sammy bawled, "Sammy don' wan' Ho-Ho-Ho come."

The kids who cheered broke into song: "You'd better watch out, you'd better not cry, you'd better not pout, I'm telling you why. . . ."

But the singing fell off when Mrs. Barnes said, "It's not going to be Santa; it's going to be a surprise guest."

"Did you hear that, Sammy? Santa's not coming," Ruth said to comfort him. But with that, three of the other young ones burst into tears.

"What's wrong now?" Mr. Barnes asked.

"Ruthie said Santa's not coming," Morgan said between sobs.

Mr. Barnes stroked Morgan's head and said, "Let's try this again. We will have a guest for Christmas dinner who does not have a white beard and isn't even from this country."

Morgan looked up and asked hopefully, "Is he from the North Pole?"

"He's from Africa. He's visiting churches in our area and, because I'm president of the church council, he will spend part of Christmas with us."

●

"I'll bet you didn't have Christmas when you were a boy," Morgan boasted.

"Oh, yes, of course I did," Mr. Mosi replied, admiring the Christmas tree and poking at the roots that were hidden under a large scarf.

"In Africa? Really? I didn't think the missionaries got there until just a little while ago," Ruth suggested.

"There are many Christians in Africa, perhaps more than in North America, I think."

Ruth slid two freshly wrapped packages under the tree as she said, "So you were raised as a Christian?"

"My, yes," he replied. "My own grandmother— who is now 93 years old—has been a Christian for over 80 years. She raised us to love the Lord."

"I had no idea. So how do you celebrate Christmas in your country?" Ruth could tell she had asked the right question because Mr. Mosi's smile became broader and softer.

"It is very beautiful. There is no electricity in my home church so on Christmas eve we all come to church very late with candles and lanterns. And we sing many wonderful songs that night."

"How can you read the words of the hymns without electricity?" Mick asked.

Mr. Mosi explained, "We rarely use hymnals at all. You see, everybody learns all the verses by heart from the time we are young . . . sometimes as many as 20 verses to a single hymn!"

"Twenty verses!" Mick exclaimed. "You'd have time for only a couple of hymns and a short sermon."

"Oh, our Christmas eve service goes on for three hours with more than one sermon, and even then people really don't want to go home when it is over."

"Do you open presents?" Mick asked.

"Presents? Yes, I guess we also have presents, but they are not as many as you have in America. I think presents are very important here," Mr. Mosi suggested.

"Important?" Mick thought that sounded like the understatement of the century. "Some of my friends don't even bother to come to church on Christmas so they can stay home to play with their presents."

"Indeed?" Mr. Mosi clicked his tongue very fast. "How can they be happy when they do such a thing? How can they give the Christ child a gift?"

"Do you do that? Give Jesus a gift at Christmas?" Mick asked.

"Of course," he replied, "and I see that you plan to give Christ Jesus the same gift as I."

Mick looked at the carpet. *Should I tell him that we don't do that in this country?* he wondered.

Mr. Mosi pointed at the packages and then swept his arm around to point at himself. "You and I give the same gift to Jesus this year, Mick, except my gift is wrapped in a different color package than yours. My gift is dark brown," he said pinching the skin on his arm. "Your gift is light brown. Isn't that the best gift of all?"

Mr. Mosi's prayer: *Thank you for putting me with a family this year for Christmas that thinks more about Jesus Christ than about presents. They are very wise in how they celebrate Christmas. And Lord, bless my own family with your presence; that is the best present of all! Amen.*

Action idea: Christmas is Jesus' birthday celebration, you know. Think of a creative way your family can give gifts to honor Jesus on his birthday this year.

"The King will reply, 'I tell you, whenever you did this for one of the least important of these brothers of mine, you did it for me!"
—Matthew 25:40 TEV

●

"We are all part of the village family . . . and that is worth much more than an ocean of mud."

Squishing Cousins

Samueli searched the stream bed until he found a glossy, white stone half the size of his little finger. He tied one end of a 10-foot length of string to the stone. Then he threw the stone back into the frigid water that had come from the glaciers atop the great African volcano, Mount Kilimanjaro.

Samueli pulled on the string, easing the bright stone across the pebbles and sand on the bottom of the stream.

"Not too slowly, not too fast," he muttered in Swahili.

A large claw reached out from under a flat rock and grasped the stone at the end of the string.

"Not too slowly, not too fast," Samueli said once again with feeling. He pulled smoothly, knowing that fast, jerky movements would scare the fresh-water crab away, but that slow movements would cause the crab to lose interest.

The crab, suspended by his own curious claw and nothing more, was lifted through the water and into the air.

"Not too slowly, not too fast," Samueli said again as he dropped the crab into the waiting basket. "That is the important thing."

An hour later, with eight crabs in the basket already, Samueli was oh-so-carefully pulling in yet one more when he suddenly let out a yell and slapped at his left lower leg. The crab on the string gave a jerk and fell back into the frigid water.

Samueli flashed a glance at his feet in the long grass just long enough to verify what he already knew was true: army ants!

A swarm of army ants, each almost an inch long with oversized heads and powerful pinchers, now infested the grass around him. The pinch of an army ant, he knew from painful experience, was so powerful that people actually could use its bite like stitches to close a cut. After inviting the ant to bite both sides of a cut, the person would pull the body off leaving the glossy black head with its pincher as strong in death as it had been in life.

Of course, these thoughts passed through Samueli's mind in an instant. He dashed just 10 steps away and began picking the painful invaders from his lower legs before he realized that he had left the basket of crabs on the stream's edge.

"Shenzi!" he scolded himself. "Now I've got to go back there or the family won't have crab for supper." He still might have left the crabs there had he not remembered that his grandmother had gone with the others for food for the cows and would be hungry when she returned for her favorite food, crab, something Samueli had promised her that morning.

"Ah, well," he said thoughtfully as he watched the basket from a safe distance, "is not a family worth more than a little pain? He rubbed the ankles once more, straightened, then bounded back to regain his family's supper.

•

Little Grace made the mistake of sneaking up on Samueli to pinch him just as he passed the stand of sugar cane.

"You jumped!" she cried. "I made you jump for the first time. You were really scared this time, Samueli."

"The army ants bit me today and I pulled their heads off, the crabs too have pinched me and I'm going to eat them for supper," he replied with mock seriousness, "but I haven't decided yet what to do with you, Grace."

"But remember that *ujamaa* means 'sharing,' Samueli," she replied nervously. "We are an ujamaa family who shares with love. Here, let me help you prepare the crabs."

•

"Tomorrow we begin to build the school," his father said over supper that night. Samueli, who had helped with the construction of several houses before turning 13 years of age, wondered if building a school would be different.

•

"You two! Into the mud you go," the village elder said to Samueli and his friend, Daudi. Five girls from Samueli's school, which met temporarily in the church for classes, began to snicker.

Samueli slipped as he stepped into the slick pit but caught himself with his hands. The snickers turned into guffaws.

"What are you laughing at, you girls?" he said sharply, a little embarrassed. "Don't you know that I have the most important job in building this whole school?"

"Sure," one said, "and if you are the *fundi* who will skillfully build our school, why have the adults put you in the slime pit?"

"You and Daudi have finally been put where you belong," said another. "That should teach you a lesson for playing tricks on us at school."

"We are heroes of the village because of what we do today," Daudi replied with pride.

"That's true," Samueli added. "Every brick that is used to build the school—many, many thousands of them—will come first from our mud pit before they are formed and baked hard. And after all, is not the village family worth more than a little mud?"

"Family?" the first said. "Nobody in *my* family works in the mud. We are shopkeepers and proud of it."

"Into the mud, girls," the village elder said returning to the pit. "The village family needs you."

"But. . . ."

"If you want a school, everybody must do their part," he concluded with a voice that suggested there would be no arguing.

"Is not the village family worth more than a little mud?" asked Samueli, this time with sarcasm.

"That's the spirit, Samueli," the elder replied. "I'm putting you in charge of the pit today. You decide how many and who can work together at one time. Keep the mud at just this consistency by adding water when you need to."

After the elder had returned to the group of adults who were laying out the contours of where the school would be, Samueli turned to the five girls and said, "There's room for just five in the pit, Daudi, don't you agree?"

"Now, Samueli," the first girl pleaded, "we are all part of the village family so we are your sisters. You don't make sisters go in the mud, do you?"

"Cousins!" he blurted. "You're cousins, third cousins to me, if anything." Samueli grabbed her foot with a deft move and threatened to pull her in."

"I'm coming, Cousin Samueli, but not because you say so," she answered with defiance. "We are all part of the village family . . . and that is worth much more than an ocean of mud." She leapt neatly into the center of the pit, startling the boys who lost their balance, fell backward, and splatted heavily.

As Samueli looked with an amused expression at Daudi, he said, "You know, this actually feels pretty good. It's a great way to stay cool on a hot afternoon, isn't it?"

Before mud found its way into the first brick mold, all seven kids were sitting together in the mud pit, squishing cousins of the same village family.

●

A month later, with tens of thousands of bricks formed, dried, and baked, then built deftly into a seven-room school, the village met in the evening to begin a three-day celebration of the end of their labors.

"The village family has given a gift to its children," the senior village elder said. "A new school. We have thanked each other many times, but we must also remember that money from the United States helped us to buy roofing material, windows, and a few other things that we could not build ourselves. They are part of our global village family. And, of course, we must now bow our heads to thank God, our heavenly Father who has once again shown us how to be members of his one heavenly family. With God, it is always the heavenly family that comes first. Let us pray. . . .

The elder's prayer: Oh, God our Father, you make us brothers and sisters with each other, with our family in the United States, and with you. Together we have worked a miracle creating a school from the dust of the earth just as we were made from the dust of the earth. Breathe into the school the same life that you breathed into us and keep us always a part of your eternal family, for we pray in the name of Jesus our brother. Amen.

Action idea: Write and find out how you can become part of schools being built in village families in Africa by contacting Operation Bootstrap Africa, 122 West Franklin Ave., Suite No. 216, Minneapolis, MN 55404.

"Honor your father and your mother, so that you
may live long in the land the Lord your God
is giving you."
—Exodus 20:12

•

*"Mom . . . dad . . . you're grounded for a week. It
will be a little embarrassing for you to
explain it to your employers. . . ."*
—Alvin

Rocky Is Grounded

"Where is all your money going, young man!"
Alvin's mother demanded.

"Never mind," he replied, "I don't need a raise
for my allowance that bad. Sorry I asked."

"We can talk about that raise; that's not the point.
Your dad and I were talking about raising it 25 cents
anyway." Mrs. Kirkland held up the broken ceramic
money bank. "But I want to know why the sudden
interest in money and why you broke into this. There
must have been over $20.00 in there."

"$39.01," Alvin said.

"Twice as much as I thought! Where can you
spend money like that so fast? It's not Christmas;
you're not going to camp or anything."

"I can't tell you just now," he answered.

Mrs. Kirkland winced, then swung around to leave his cluttered room, but turned once more, "If you can't tell me, then I can't trust you because it must be something I wouldn't approve of. You're grounded. For a week, at least."

Less than a minute after the door slammed shut, Theresa opened it a crack and popped her head through.

"I heard all of it," she said in an awed whisper. "You were great! Didn't crack under interrogation. What a man!"

"Yah, a regular Rocky," he replied. "Except nobody would ever dare ground Rocky."

"It's only a week, and by next Saturday they'll find out about it all, anyway."

"I suppose I can hold out."

"It's going to be worth it, keeping it a secret and all. You'll see . . . Rocky."

"Yah, right," he moaned as she pulled the door shut.

●

"We called the bank to see if you put that money in your new account, and they say you have already drawn out the $20.00 that we put in there in the first place!" Alvin's dad said from his big soft throne in the living room.

"That's not your account," Alvin said in a small voice. "You had no right—"

"I have a right to know what is going on."

"You didn't have to do it that way."

94

"What has happened to all your money?" Mr. Kirkland demanded.

"Uh. . . ."

"Your mother and I have thought of every possible reason and there is nothing going on these days that seems to us to be a legitimate reason."

"There's a good reason," Alvin said.

"What is it?"

"I can't tell you yet. I'd be giving something away that I shouldn't."

"When can you tell us?"

"That would be giving too much away, too."

"I see."

Alvin got up to go back to his room.

"You're grounded, you know," Alvin's dad said.

"I know," he replied. "For a week."

"For two weeks!"

"Right . . . two weeks."

As Alvin passed Theresa's room he heard a whispered, "Rocky II strikes again."

●

But the third time it was Theresa's turn to get chewed out.

"Theresa, there's someone on the phone for you," her mom called out.

"I'll take it up here," Theresa called from the small table at the end of the upstairs hall.

"Hi, Theresa, it's Marcus," a deep voice said on the phone.

95

When she heard who it was, she stretched the cord so the phone could be used in the bathroom and turned on the faucet.

Five minutes later, she emerged and skipped down the steps, grabbed her jacket from the closet doorknob, and pushed on the screen door to let herself out.

"Theresa, who's Marcus?" Mrs. Kirkland asked from the living room. Her mother and father were sitting together.

"You weren't listening, were you?" she asked with surprise.

"I heard the name before I hung up," her mother replied.

"You didn't hear anything else?"

"No. Who is he?"

"Just a boy," she said with relief in her voice.

"Boy! Sounded like he was at least 25 years old, Theresa," Mrs. Kirkland said.

"Who is he? Is he in college?" her father asked.

"I can't tell you, dad," Theresa said with eyes screwed shut. She knew that her answer would not be popular.

"First Alvin, then you. Didn't we raise you kids better than all this?" Mrs. Kirkland complained.

"But I'm almost 18, almost legal age to vote," she tried.

"As long as you live under our roof. . . ."

Theresa knew she would get the "roof" lecture.

"It's a matter of trust. Simple trust," her father concluded.

"We can't trust you, Theresa, if you're going to be secretive about such important things." Mrs. Kirkland, clearly uncomfortable about the whole affair, looked at Theresa directly. "I'm afraid we're going to have to ground you, too, until we can build some of that trust back up."

"It's a matter of trust. Simple trust," her father said. "This will give you time to think about trust, simple trust."

Theresa didn't even argue. It sounded too much like the railroad job that they had done on Alvin.

She clomped back up the stairs that she had only recently skipped down and passed Alvin's room on her way to her own.

It was unmistakeable. The theme song from Rocky along with a brotherly chuckle wafted through the door of Alvin's bedroom, swelling as she walked triumphantly to her own room. *It really helps,* she thought. *It's all for a reason.*

●

The next morning.

"Happy anniversary to you, happy anniversary to you, happy anniversary mom and dad, happy anniversary to you."

The song was met by four bleary eyes that belonged to Alvin's and Theresa's parents.

A huge tray with a four-course breakfast on it was laid in the center of the king-sized bed.

"This is a surprise," Mr. Kirkland said.

"Especially since our anniversary isn't for another five days," Mrs. Kirkland added.

"We know. You just kind of squeezed it out of us," said Theresa.

"What do you mean?" her mother asked.

"It's not just an anniversary coming up next Thursday," Theresa said. "It's a special one, right?"

"Our 25th," her father said with a yawn.

"Your silver anniversary, right. So Alvin and Rick and I went in together on a gift . . . but, of course, Rick won't be able to come home until next weekend. Alvin and I called him late last night to see if it was all right if we gave you our gift now."

"We got tired of being grounded, so he said it was all right," Alvin said.

Both parents' mouths were hanging open as if something was just beginning to dawn on them.

"So we want to give this envelope to you both," Alvin finished.

"All your money—" his mother began.

"Most of it went into the gift," Alvin said.

"And that guy on the phone—"

"He's the young travel agent at Aderly Travel Agency," Theresa replied. "He said the tickets were ready, but since I am grounded you'll have to settle for a note explaining everything."

"Tickets . . . oh, dear."

She opened the envelope.

"Hawaii!" they both exclaimed.

"We have been so unfair without knowing the whole story," Mr. Kirkland said.

"It's a matter of trust, simple trust," Theresa suggested. "This trip will give you time to think about trusting Alvin and me a little better."

"We will, honey," her dad replied. "We will."

The two parents pulled the two kids past the eggs and bacon and toast and fruit and cereal and coffee on the tray with the flower vase and gave them big hugs.

"We really have had rocks in our heads," Mrs. Kirkland said.

"True," Alvin added.

"What can we do to make things up to you both?"

"I've been thinking about that," Alvin answered. "Mom . . . dad . . . you're grounded for a week. It will be a little embarrassing for you to explain it to your employers and you'll have to give us the keys to the car so we can get groceries, but—"

The pillow caught Alvin square in the face.

As he lay under its fluffiness, he found himself humming the theme from Rocky. He added his own commentary: *"Rocky takes it on the jaw. He's down . . . but not out!"*

Alvin's prayer: I forgive them, Lord, because they didn't know what they were doing. Amen.

Action idea: Look up Luke 23:32-34. Who else prayed the prayer that Alvin prayed above? Is there anything about Alvin's story that reminded you of the story in Luke 23?

"The Lord your God has chosen you out of all the peoples on the face of the earth to be his people, his treasured possession."
—Deuteronomy 7:6b

•

"This typxwritxr makxs mx so angry that I want to clobbxr it!"
—Mick

A Lxttxr to God

Dxar God,

I comx from a rxally big family. Thxrx arx sxvxn boys and thrxx girls in my family, not counting mom and dad. You probably know all thxir namxs so I won't borx you with thx dxtails.

Anyway, somxtimxs I usxd to think that if I wxrxn't around it wouldn't mattxr to anyonx. I thought I was just onx morx mouth to fxxd and not vxry important.

Oncx, my family was on a trip out wxst. My mom drovx thx station wagon and my dad drovx thx campxr trailxr. Xvxn with all that room it was still crowdxd. And with all of us kids togxthxr on that long trip wx must havx stoppxd at xvxry gas station on Intxrstatx 90.

Aftxr wx had stoppxd for about thx 15th timx, I

101

was sitting on thx bumpxr of thx Winnxbago whxn I hxard mom comx up to dad's window—thxy couldn't sxx mx—and say, "Don't you wish wx had a fxw lxss of thxm about now?" I couldn't bxlixvx my xars! It wasn't our fault wx wxrx born. I got mad.

Wxll, thrxx stops latxr, wx wxrx sitting in a park along thx highway xating our lunch whxn I just had to go, you know, to thx rxstroom. Xvxryonx but mom and Sammy wxrx playing touch football in thx play arxa, so, whilx mom was ovxr scraping things into thx garbagx, I told Sammy (who just turnxd two yxars old) that I was going to thx rxstroom. Sammy smilxd and said, "Wxstwoom," so I knxw hx got thx mxssagx. I guxss hx just forgot to txll anyonx.

To makx a long story short, thxy lxft mx thxrx!! I didn't takx a long timx in thx rxstroom or anything! Thxy just took off bxforx I got out. It wouldn't havx madx mx vxry mad, in fact I would havx thought it was funny xxcxpt that I had just hxard mom say to dad, "Don't you wish wx had a fxw lxss of thxm about now?" I actually wondxrxd for a fxw minutxs if thxy had lxft mx on purposx and plannxd to gxt rid of us onx by onx on thxir way wxst.

It was xmbarrassing. Pxoplx kxpt coming up to mx and asking if I was lost. "No," I said to thxm, "I know xxactly whxrx I am." I didn't want to admit what my own parxnts had donx. Finally, just to havx a good rxason to bx thxrx, I told a truck drivxr that I was out at thx highway park to makx somx monxy washing windshixlds.

A Lxttxr to God

Hx had mx wash his windshixld thxn and thxrx with papxr towxls from thx rxstroom, and, bxforx you know it, I was washing morx and morx. Thx good nxws is that I madx ovxr $20 washing windshixlds. I couldn't bxlixvx it. Thx bad nxws is that I madx that much bxcausx it took my parxnts and brothxrs and sistxrs thrxx hours and two potty stops bxforx thxy discovxrxd that thxy had lxft mx at thx highway park!

You don't know what wxnt through my hxad as I waitxd and hopxd that thxy would comx back for mx and txll mx it was an accidxnt. I fxxl xspxcially guilty that I wondxrxd if I xvxn mattxrxd to you, God. If I could gxt lost in a family of a dozxn, how could I possibly bx worth anything to you who havx billions of pxoplx to watch ovxr. Arx thxrx xvxr timxs whxn you say to yoursxlf, "Don't you wish wx had a fxw lxss of thxm about now?"

Anyway, until my family showxd up again, I thought I wasn't worth anything to anybody xxcxpt to thx truck drivxrs with dirty windshixlds.

Now that I look back on it, it was rxally funny to sxx thx look on mom's and dad's facxs whxn thxy finally found mx. Thxy showxd mx that thxy hadn't mxant to gxt rid of mx by all thx hugs and kissxs and xvxn txars. It was a littlx xmbarrassing in front of thx truckxrs, to bx honxst with you. Thxn, I got to sit in thx swivxl sxat nxxt to dad all thx way out wxst; I had my own window and xvxrything!

So, I guxss I am spxcial in my family, xvxn though it is so big.

103

And I think that xvxry pxrson must bx spxcial to you, too, God. I am lxarning that xvxn a singlx thing out of placx can rxally bx noticxablx. For instancx, thx "x" on this stupid xlxctronic typxwritxr nxvxr comxs out as an "x" but is always printxd as an "X." (It's so scrxwxd up that I can't xvxn txll you how scrxwxd up it is without it scrxwing up.) It's just onx of thx 72 kxys on this thing, but do I xvxr noticx whxn thx onx lxttxr isn't thxrx! It makxs mx think that you would noticx if xvxn onx of your pxoplx was hurting or not whxrx hx was supposxd to bx. Wxll, thank you for listxning.

Gotta go!

Lovx,
Mick Barnxs

Mick's prayxr: Is it wrong to bx angry? This typxwritxr makxs mx so angry that I want to clobbxr it! Thank you for turning my anger into love. I feel loved by you and by my family. I don't think I'll ever feel like I did at the highway park again. Amen. P.S. When I clobbered this typewriter I think I fixed it!

Action idea: Go wash the windshield of every car in your garage or driveway and leave a note for the owner telling them God loves them.

"And we know that in all things God works for the good of those who love him, who have been called according to his purpose."
—Romans 8:28

•

"It's amazing. God even made something good come out of being humiliated at the cafe. And she's really cute."
—Billy

Too Much Too Loud

"Why aren't you out playing with your friends?"

Billy hated it when his mother asked him questions that he didn't know how to answer.

What should I say? *Nobody likes me, everybody hates me, I think I'll go eat worms?*

"I'm sticking around while grandpa is still here. He'll be leaving in a few days."

"Grandpa wouldn't mind if you take off after lunch for a few hours," she said. "Would you, dad?"

Billy's mind whirled. *I don't know anybody in town yet well enough to just walk up to their house and ask if such-and-such can come out to play. Besides, I don't "play" anymore. I'm too big for that,* Billy thought. *And I haven't met anyone at school in this dinky town because school hasn't started yet. Maybe I can go to the*

*park and collect aluminum cans or something just to get
out of the house. . . .*

"Actually, Billy has already promised to go with
me to the cafe uptown for lunch," grandpa called
out from his easy chair.

Billy brightened. At least it would be something
to do so mother doesn't start calling the neighbors
to see if there's a "little friend" for me.

"Let's go, grandpa," Billy offered. "Sounds
great!"

"But, dad, my stew will be done in half an hour."

*Mom knows how to whine to get her way like I do
sometimes to get my way. I know where I learned it
from,* thought Billy.

"Why didn't you tell me you two were planning
that, Billy?"

"Slipped my mind, I guess," he answered. *It really
has slipped my mind. I wonder when we talked about
that. . . .*

"And you know me, June," grandpa said loudly,
"my memory is getting weaker every day."

"I'm Linda, father," Billy's mom answered with
more than a hint of irritation. "June lives in Texas,
remember?"

"Oh, yes . . . see what I mean? Ready to go,
Billy?"

●

". . . and I'll have the veal cutlet with mashed
potatoes and a cup of your soup," grandpa said in
his booming voice. Heads turned to see who the voice

belonged to, then everyone went back to their own meals.

The waitress gathered the menus and went to get their water.

"Grandpa, when did we agree to go out for lunch?" Billy asked.

"I forget," grandpa said with a wink.

"We didn't, did we . . . ?"

"Not really, no."

"Then why did you say so? I mean, I think it's great, but . . . why are you making up stories to fake out mom?"

"I didn't do it for that reason. I did it to get you out of the house."

"Really? Why?"

"Because you didn't know what to do with yourself today and your mother doesn't understand that yet."

People looked over from their own tables again.

He's pretty smart, Billy thought. *It's like he can read my mind. But I wish he would keep his voice down a bit.*

"How do you know that?" Billy asked.

"Same way as I know you're writing letters to that pretty blonde girl back in Rock Port . . . what's her name?"

Heads turned again to look at the owner of the deep voice. Billy slid down in the booth.

"Grandpa! Shhh!! How do you know these things? I've only written twice."

"Same way as I know—"

"Shhhhhhhh . . . !!! Grandpa, I'll leave if you don't keep it down." Billy clutched at his jacket in case he had to leave suddenly.

Billy noticed that two tables of people sitting nearby were totally silent. *That's a bit unusual considering that they haven't even gotten their food yet. They're listening. That one man is even leaning this direction. Nosey!*

Thankfully, the waitress brought the soup and glasses of water.

"Got a quarter, grandpa?"

"Sure."

Billy took the coin and deposited it in the small jukebox vender just above the salt and pepper shakers on the wall. He pressed the first two buttons he came to: D-3.

At least now we'll have some background noise so people can't listen to us as well. Guitars twanged and a cowboy sang:

> "Oh, they call me city slicker
> but I sure know how to pick 'er
> that ol' country gal and a
> six-string steel guitar . . ."

Once again, heads turned, this time a couple of faces wearing scowls, as people tried to discover who had picked the song.

Billy concentrated on his soup.

The rest of the meal was mostly uneventful, but Billy noticed that he ended up chewing on the sticks from his corn dogs longer than usual.

"That was a fine meal," his grandpa said as he scooped up the last bit of gravy with his bread.

"Yes, thanks for taking me along."

"Anytime. You know, I'm going to have to learn to be quieter in public," he said, once again too loudly. "I think I'll pray more and talk less."

Billy said, "That would be quieter, grandpa."

"Gonna pray that you get some friends!" he said, pounding the table.

This time grandpa had gone too far. Everybody in the cafe turned in their seats and looked straight at them, including a girl with pretty blond hair that reminded Billy of. . . .

Billy grabbed his jacket and mumbled, "I'm going to the restroom. I'll meet you out front."

He hustled off, trying not to stumble as people watched his every move.

●

"Thank you, sir, come again," the waitress said to grandpa at the counter.

"Oh, I will now that my daughter and her family moved to town," he boomed.

"Are they new here?"

Billy pushed out into the street.

Before the door had fully closed, the blonde girl came out and stood just to his right side.

"I'm new, too," she said with confidence.

"Oh," was all Billy could muster.

"I couldn't help hearing that you are new to town," she tried again.

*And that I don't have any friends here and that I'm
writing to someone back in Rock Port.*

"School starts in a week," she said.

"I know."

"What grade will you be in?"

"Seventh."

"Same here."

"Really?"

"Yup! And I like country and western music like
you, too."

Billy thought about the city slicker song and lied,
"I do too."

"I know you do."

"Maybe I'll see you at school next week."

"For sure."

Grandpa came outside, took Billy by the shoulder
and led him to the car.

"Grandpa," Billy said as they were both getting
inside, "you're not hard of hearing. Why were you
talking so loud in there?"

"Pretty girl you met just there. Bet she's also going
to be in the seventh grade. . . . I'm sorry, were you
saying something?"

"Grandpa, how do you know these things?" Billy
realized he wasn't going to get a straight answer, so
he concentrated on not staring at the pretty blonde
girl as they drove past her. He couldn't help but
notice that she waved a very private wave.

Billy's prayer: *Help me some day to be smart about
people like grandpa is. He seems to understand without
even trying. Amen.*

Action idea: Take a shot at writing the words to a song about friends. Use it with a familiar melody that you borrow from another song or make up your own.